THROUGH TROUBLED WATERS

Overcoming the Challenges of Being Bullied and Teased

Pam Turner

as told to Ken Hinkley

WESTBOW
P R E S S
A DIVISION OF THOMAS NELSON

All Scripture quotations are from THE HOLY BIBLE, NEW INTERNATIONAL VERSION ®, NIV® copyright © 1973, 1978, 1989, 2011 by Biblica, Inc™. Used by permission. All rights reserved worldwide.

WestBow Press books may be ordered through booksellers or by contacting:

WestBow Press
A Division of Thomas Nelson
1663 Liberty Drive
Bloomington, IN 47403
www.westbowpress.com
1-(866) 928-1240

ISBN: 978-1-4497-4036-8 (sc)
ISBN: 978-1-4497-4038-2 (hc)
ISBN: 978-1-4497-4037-5 (e)

Library of Congress Control Number: 2012902531

Printed in the United States of America

WestBow Press rev. date: 02/15/2012

To my grandmother,

Thelma B. Houghton,

Without whose influence and prayers I might have drifted onto the rocks of death a long time ago.

Introduction

Bullying and teasing are age old problems that should have been done away with long ago but are still with us today. This new book gives an inside view of the damage they can do to a person at each and every stage of life. It does not matter where bullying or teasing comes from – it is bad for a person's sense of personhood. This well written account (with study guide questions at the end of each chapter) is a must read for any person young or old – either from a faith based or secular based point of view. It is very timely and much needed in the secular world as well as in Christian circles.

Rev. Richard Freeman

Pastor

Foreword

God's wonderful provision and loving hand is well illustrated through the pages of Pam's life. This book will resonate in the life of the reader as we all have experienced similar type-casting and have either been on the receiving end of sub sequential abuse or have perpetrated abuse ourselves.

Those with disabilities receive harsher treatment and are misunderstood, especially in their childhood years.

Pam openly shares her special needs and resulting hardships and abuse, not only to tell her story, but to benefit those who find themselves on either side of the issues put forth in this book.

I also challenge the reader to look for God's loving hand through Pam's walk. Her life is a success story and will hopefully lead others to the same conclusion – love others as Jesus loves you.

Alan Hutchinson

Music Pastor

Peru Baptist Church

Preface

This book was written, first, as a means to tell Pam's story and hopefully get more people to be aware of the negative impact of the way we treat one another, especially those with handicaps or special needs. It was intended to be a wake-up call.

As we worked on the project, it became clear to us that there are many others who are calling for more equal treatment of one another and perhaps our book might be just one more voice competing to be heard. So we went back, took a look at what we had done, and asked, "How can we make this more practical and helpful and not just another biography?" After much prayer and discussion, we decided that to engage the reader, we would list discussion questions. These are designed to get readers, as individuals or in small groups, to think about the subject matter of the chapter they have just read and how the incidences in Pam's life may be reflected in the lives of others. Some of the questions are intentionally challenging so the reader will not leave with a "so what?" attitude.

We also added a few paragraphs that deal with specific reactions to bullying, taunting, and teasing. These are informative pages to help make the reader aware of facts and feelings that perhaps would not come to their attention otherwise.

By the grace of God, we hope we have succeeded in providing a resource that is not only entertaining, but useful as a discussion guide and an information source for individuals, teachers, and group leaders.

It should be noted that any names used in the "Let's Talk" sections are purely fictional and do not represent any real person that we know of.

So, dear reader, we take you on a journey through some difficult waters that you cannot navigate alone. Find a friend or two, talk to your group leader, or read it together as a family. We believe that if you do this, there will be no way you could ever see a person with disabilities the same way again. God bless.

Ken Hinkley

Chapter One

The Early Years

His disciples went down to the lake, where they got into
a boat and set off across the lake.

John 6:16–17 NIV

I am nine years old. For as long as I can remember, I have felt like an outsider. No one really understands me or the difficulties I face every day. I go to school, but I don't enjoy it or learn very much.

Thinking back to those days makes me wonder why it took so long for someone to realize I had a problem. I had difficulty seeing the board, reading posters, or focusing on artwork hung on the walls. Because of that, I was seated at the front of the class, where other "problem" children sat so the teacher could monitor their attention more closely. Maybe everyone thought all I had was a vision problem, but it was really more than that.

What no one else could understand was that even when I could see the material, it didn't always make sense to me. I had difficulty reading words or understanding the words I read. Ideas and concepts that came easily to others my own age were a struggle for me. I hated to read aloud because of my difficulty with pronunciation. Sometimes I would read a paragraph over and over before I understood what was being said. So I quietly suffered and bluffed my way through the early grades. But I knew it wouldn't last forever.

One day our teacher, Mrs. Francis, asked me to read out loud. I refused. I did not want to embarrass myself in front of the entire class. These kids were my neighbors, and I knew that I would not be left alone once they found out I could not read well. The teacher, however, thought my refusal was an act of rebellion. She assumed I was defying her authority, and consequently I was punished for it.

In spite of her desire to see us succeed, Mrs. Francis had her limits, like any other person. As a group of special-needs kids, we often pushed her to those limits. I remember that one day I did something that she felt needed correction, so she grabbed me firmly by the shoulder to move me from my place to another point in the room. I didn't like that, so I yelled at her, grabbed my coat, and ran the half mile to my home.

When I showed my mother the finger marks, I got the attention of my parents. They were naturally upset, but only for a short time. Soon the incident was behind us and life went on.

The playground was a nightmare. Physically, it was plenty large enough for the students' needs for physical activity, but it would never be large enough to escape their torments, teasing, and bullying. I was often called "retarded." There was a lot of "accidental" shoving in the hallways or in line.

Because of the negative attitudes of others, I spent a lot of time by myself.

Since they did not want me around, I was not asked to join them very often, but I chose to be alone equally as often.

Many times I would not even go outside. I would find a place in a corner of the school to stay by myself to avoid their taunts. Our teacher and other staff would try to encourage me to join the other kids, but no one ever asked me why I desired to be alone. On the days I did venture outside, I always felt unwanted and unaccepted, and I was usually the last to be chosen for any team activity.

From time to time I would try to participate, but usually got the same response:

"We don't want a retard on our team!"

"You can't play good enough."

"Go back to your corner and leave us alone."

Rejection wasn't limited to the school playground, however. At home it seemed like my siblings would rather play with each other or by themselves than with me. Even they sometimes picked on me or teased me. Being family, they actually took things a step further, knowing they could get away with more.

One of my sisters was upset with me one day because I wanted to play what she and some of the other siblings were playing. She didn't want me there, so she threw a rock at me when I wasn't looking and split my head open.

Another time, when we were chasing each other through the house, another sister didn't want me to follow her so she slammed a door, thinking it would just keep me out, but I had already put my hand on the doorway and a finger was crushed. She said she was not sorry and maybe it would teach me a lesson. I still carry the scars from these and other similar incidents.

Then there was the time when we were all down at the swimming hole in the river near our house. I couldn't swim very well, so I was playing on the rocks and having fun with the others. Next thing I knew, one of my cousins pushed me in. No one tried to help me out. I had to fight my way to the edge and climb out by myself.

My sister Delores, however, often stood up for me against the others. I was probably closer to her than any other of my brothers and sisters. Years later, it was learned that she had similar problems. Thus, perhaps it was true empathy on her part. She would know more than anyone else what I was going through.

Because of my negative self-image, by the time I had reached fifth grade my test scores had slipped even lower than they were previously. They were not outstanding to begin with, but now they bordered on failure.

One day I expressed the desire to stay home and not go to school. When my mother questioned me, I said that I would be no worse off at home than at school, where I was misunderstood and teased mercilessly. She asked about my experiences and feelings. We discussed the options of staying home versus going back. In my emotionally distressed state, I could see no benefit to either option. But Mother would not give up on me.

She called the school and insisted on meeting with the school staff to find out why I was acting the way I was and doing so poorly in my studies. The result was about a week of intense testing of all sorts. There were dexterity tests: stacking blocks; matching colors, shapes, and forms; and other similar things. There were mental skills review, such as flash cards relating to math, spelling, reading, and comprehension. Some of the tests were oral, but I was also asked to write sentences and a short paragraph on a given subject. Each test, as I remember, lasted one to two hours. It was a real torture to endure all this mental concentration. But I did it, and it was helpful. It was discovered that I had a learning disability as well as speech impairment. Finally, there was a reason why I performed so poorly and did not want to interact socially. This double affliction was what was holding me back and setting me apart from others at school.

One result from the testing was that a personal tutor was provided for me. This lady came to the school about twice a week to work with children who were having difficulties. She was a big help to me academically, but didn't really draw me out socially.

I didn't realize it then, but looking back, I now know that my handicaps triggered my withdrawal from interacting with others. I was conscious of how I was different and didn't want others to see me that way, so I kept to myself rather than put up with the teasing. On the other hand, because I was so withdrawn, it exaggerated my condition more than was necessary. I knew in my head and in my heart that I was not as slow as most believed. I just needed to learn to apply myself. It was a situation of one aspect of my condition playing off the other, back and forth, with no expectation of getting out of the dilemma.

There were many times while I was sitting alone at school during recess or off by myself after school at home that I would talk to myself. It was not really self-pity, but conversations about all sorts of things. What I remember most about those self-talks is that I knew I was important. I knew I was better than other people thought. Reflecting back on it now, I wonder if God was speaking to me even then. Perhaps He was.

All I knew for certain was that I couldn't wait to move up to the sixth grade and go to Dixfield for classes. Perhaps in a new school with larger classes and new teachers who cared, I would have a new beginning and things would be better. One could always hope.

*We are hard pressed on every side, but not crushed;
perplexed, but not in despair; persecuted, but not
abandoned; struck down, but not destroyed.*

2 Cor. 4:8–9 NIV

Discussion **Questions**

1. What was it like at your school when you were nine years old?

2. Did you observe any teasing, bullying, or verbal abuse?

3. Did you ever participate in any such activity?

4. Were you ever the victim?

5. In the Bible, read James 3:7–8. How is verbal abuse like deadly poison?

6. Have you known anyone in the lower grades who had a learning difficulty? How did you relate to that person?

7. Are adults slower to recognize handicaps than children?

8. How did you feel when you read about the teacher's attitude and actions?

9. Are there teachers like that today?

10. Do you agree with the statement that family members believe they can get away with more than nonfamily?

11. Do you believe there is a direct relationship between bullying (and other forms of abuse) and school grades? If so, how does it make a difference?

12. Pam says that she knew in her mind she was better than what other people thought of her. Is that attitude common among people in her situation?

13. At the end of Chapter One, what did Pam pin her hopes on? Was that practical?

14. In the Bible, read Psalm 39: 7–8. How does this fit Pam's situation? How does it fit yours?

15. Do we sometimes long for a new beginning?

16. In the Bible, read John 3: 1–21, 36. How was it shown that we can have a new beginning?

17. Have you started over through faith in Jesus?

Let's Talk

about using our tongues

Pam speaks about having been the victim of misunderstandings and taunting, teasing, and name-calling from an early age. For her as a child, there seemed to be no escape from those things, and they adversely affected her relationship with other people. Victims know that words hurt, but those who use hurtful words are not always aware of the level of pain they inflict on the ones they tease, taunt, or bully.

Our tongues were given to us from God as a means of communication. We are gifted in a way that is unique in creation. Unfortunately, the uniqueness is nothing to brag about. It is the means by which we diminish the value of one another. All other species on earth are designed to protect, nurture, and promote the species, even through their own communication system. Humans, however, also use it against one another to drag individuals down, to set one person or group over another, or to intimidate certain members of our society.

The reason for this is so simple: We are the only species of God's creation that has a spiritual element built into our lives. The Bible calls this "being in the image of God." When God created the first humans, He set before them a test: they could obey Him and live in peace, harmony, and without sorrow or pain—or they could disobey and go their own way and reap the consequences. This is called "sin." As we all know, they chose to sin rather than obey. Since then, every person ever born is born with that natural instinct to sin. We want what we want with little regard to the feelings and harm to others.

This is what causes us to say things about other people or to certain folks that are negative, unkind, and potentially hurtful. We see them as people who don't quite measure up to what we expect or they do not do, say, or act the way we think they should, and so we treat them unkindly.

But just because we were born with a sinful nature does not excuse us. We are still responsible for how we treat people. Intentionally saying hurtful words is a choice we make. We must then also accept the consequences of our words. If the result is making a child cry or causing children physical harm, whose fault is it? It is the fault of the one who said the things that brought the negative results. If the result is withdrawal, depression, or suicide, whose fault is it? The responsibility falls on the one or ones who tormented the victim over a period of time, sometimes many years.

The use of our tongues is a heavy responsibility. Most of us do not realize how powerful our words are. That is why the Bible warns us to be very careful how we use our verbal skills. The apostle James says it is much like starting a fire. It usually starts with a small spark (one caustic remark), and then, first thing you know, there is a fire raging out of control (a broken relationship, uncontrolled anger, a death). The truth is we don't know the extent of the damage a single word of criticism may cause.

On the other hand, the great missionary evangelist Paul says we should be using our voices to encourage and build up one another. He says words like compassion, kindness, humility, gentleness, love, and patience should describe the way we treat one another. He understood the power of praise. When we treat people the way they should be treated, they will grow and develop into people who have self-confidence, hope, and a bright future.

Jesus put it another way. We should treat others the same way we would want to be treated. If you do not like to be called names, then don't call other people names. If you don't like to be put down because your thoughts or ideas sound silly to someone else, then do not put down other people's thoughts and ideas even if they sound silly. If you do not appreciate being pushed around, do not push others into making decisions or doing things they may not want to do.

The people in Pam's life probably never realized how much they damaged her as a person by saying the things they said. Most people don't understand the power of the spoken word, either negatively or positively. If they did, more of us would follow the advice of Paul and focus on the positive because it would make things so much better for us all.

Now, we can't change the world by offering this advice. All we can do is to ask you: Do you now understand the power you have inside your mouth? Do you understand you hold the power to kill, maim, or destroy, as well as the power to build up, encourage, and help? The choice is yours. What will you do with your tongue?

Chapter Two

Junior High and Puberty

A strong wind was blowing and the waters grew rough.

John 6:18 NIV

The next fall I found out things *were* different in the Dixfield School. In addition to larger class sizes, there was much more space—more space for learning, more space for recreational and sports activities, and more space for me to be alone.

There were also opportunities to make new friends. Normally, a person gets to know classmates by talking with them, discovering things you have in common, and building relationships on those common elements. For me it happened in different and surprising ways.

One time, I witnessed an older student picking on another, younger student. Knowing the hurt feelings and shame experienced by the victim, I interfered and tried to fight off the bully.

"Leave him alone!" I shouted.

"Make me" was the threatening reply.

Words soon turned into pushing and shoving. One of us grabbed the other. We both ended up in a water puddle.

I didn't win the wrestling match, but my actions got the attention of the other students. It spread all over campus that I was not one to mess with and I would go to bat for anyone else whom I thought was being mistreated. Perhaps it was at that time I became an advocate for the underdog.

The bullying didn't stop and the shunning didn't go away, but there was a new respect for what I had done and was willing to do to guard the dignity of my fellow classmates.

To add to my self-satisfaction, I was introduced to sports. Someone asked me to join a group that wanted to play kickball.

I was suspicious at first, but joined right in and had a good time. I surprised them by how good I was. I surprised myself as well. This made me feel good because now I had found something I was good at. It didn't help much with my social skills off the field, but my self-respect was lifted a notch.

Another opportunity to become more accepted came through the specialized classes I attended in junior high. It was here, especially in reading class, that I realized that I was not alone in my condition of struggling with reading, comprehension, and social interaction. There were others in similar situations. It was in this atmosphere that I became more comfortable and open with my classmates. It was among fellow students who struggled that I felt accepted.

Reading class consisted of only six or seven students at a time. This gave us each more personal attention from the teacher and more personal interaction among ourselves. This made me less embarrassed when I took my turn to read aloud. I was also much less rebellious. Outside of this group, others often caused me to feel frustrated and misunderstood. This usually led to outbursts of anger.

I remember banging my fists on the desk in front of me because the person I was trying to communicate with was showing me no patience and had blocked out everything I was saying. It felt like I was talking to someone who wanted his own way instead of listening to what I wanted to tell him. The inability to communicate well made me angry. The devil will often take control of the weak. He certainly had me then and used me to hurt others through my anger.

Another time I got angry was when I was playing kickball during recess and was called out at first base when I was clearly safe. The student acting as an umpire didn't like me because of my handicap, so I was called out to prove a point. In my anger, I threw the ball hard. It landed beyond the edge of the field in some bushes and someone had to retrieve it before the game could go on.

There were other forms of violence I used as well to vent my frustration, but here in this classroom, I was less prone to vent my feelings in that way. Feeling accepted and equal with the others allowed me to express myself in calmer, more constructive ways.

I wanted so much to excel and gain the approval of my teachers, my fellow students, and my family. I had to really work hard at my schoolwork to bring my grades up. I felt this was one way I could show others I could succeed. I took special care to at least try to complete my homework (though I didn't always succeed) and practice my reading and math whenever I could.

Class time was not always productive, however. The special needs students did not always have long attention spans and things did not always progress according to our teacher's plan or desire. There were times when we, as a class, did not want to

study or pay attention to our lessons. Often someone would start shooting spitballs, thinking the teacher didn't see. And, once they started flying, I had to join in. I don't know if it is really true, but it seems like I was the one caught more often than the others. Other than a stern reprimand, though, there were no real consequences to such episodes. On the other hand, it did show our lack of discipline when it came to studies.

Studying and playing kickball were not the only things I learned to do while in junior high. It was here that I was given a level of work responsibility. Opportunities opened up to help the lunchroom crew with cleaning up the dining hall during and after lunch each day. Students were offered a free lunch if we would keep the trash picked up, the floors clean, and the tables washed. I did these things with enthusiasm and joy. Not only was I doing something productive, but it gave me more time to enjoy my own thoughts and to avoid interaction with those students who

treated me badly. For the most part, it was a comfortable atmosphere, which pleased me well.

Even there, however, there were times when the other kids picked on me or deliberately did things that were hurtful and mean. I can't tell you how many times I found messes on the tables, chairs, or floor that someone made just because they knew I was on cleanup duty.

One student says, "I don't want my pudding. You want my pudding? Ooops! I spilled it on the table. That's okay; Pam's on duty today. She can clean it up."

Another takes his tray toward the counter and drops it just before he gets there. "Pam! There's a mess over here. Can you clean it up?" He laughs as he leaves the room.

Then when I was almost done with the cafeteria cleaning and about to leave, someone comes walking in on the floor I just mopped before it has a chance to dry.

"What are you doing? Get off my clean floor!"

"I'm just getting something real quick" or "I have to; I forgot something I need for class" were the usual answers. It didn't matter what their excuse was. I still had to go behind them and wipe up the tracks.

Having experienced success at kickball, I was eager to try other physical activities. At some point, someone unknown to us erected a chin-up bar in our classroom. Don't ask me why it was there. All I know is that it tempted me to see if I could do it. I always did love a challenge. The result was that I did as well as or better than some of the boys! Score another point for me!

I don't want to make it sound like I was alone all the time. I wasn't. I did have a few people I could hang out with and call my friends. I still remember Ruth, who was probably the one I was closest to during my school days. Ruth was the kind of person everyone should have as a friend. She was kind and compassionate toward everyone. She had the ability to listen and make you feel she understood. I believe she *did* understand a lot of my difficulties, since she also faced many of the same challenges. She was also not afraid to stand up to someone who was bullying another student. She was not one to stand by and say nothing. In other words, she was a lot like me. Maybe that's why I liked her and we got along so well together.

Often we would visit each other's homes. I probably spent more time at her house than she did at mine, though. Her parents were very welcoming to me and even put me up overnight a few times when we got back late from a game that took us out of town. When we got back to their house, I would call home and ask my mom if it was okay to stay with Ruth that night and go to school with her the next day. Mom always said yes because she knew Ruth's parents would take good care of me and she had her hands full with my siblings at home.

One other highlight in my junior high career was the eighth-grade field day.

At this annual event, the whole school participated in one sport or another. Each participant was awarded points according to how well they did. I worked hard, played hard, and enjoyed myself as the day progressed. I was racking up the points with each event, but not really paying attention to the standings. When the overall winner was announced, I was shocked to learn that it was me! I had accumulated over one hundred points throughout the day and came out on top. Wow, did that feel good! Especially since some of the other participants played on the school athletic teams.

Reflecting back on all the blessings of encouragement I received during those three years makes me think perhaps it was God's way of showing me that I was valuable, even though I was different from others. This value was reinforced by other people as well. My grandmother Houghton, for example, often took me to church and talked to me about being special in God's sight. She would say how much God loves each of us and everyone is equal to Him. It was through her influence that I had most of my knowledge of God or awareness that He cared. I praise God that she was there because it was partly those facts about God that got me through the tough times of junior high, puberty, and growing up with handicaps.

If the Lord had not been on our side when men attacked us, when their anger flared against us, they would have swallowed us alive; the flood would have engulfed us, the torrent would have swept over us, the raging waters would have swept us away. Praise be to the Lord, who has not let us be torn by their teeth. We have escaped like a bird out of the fowler's snare, the snare has been broken and we have escaped. Our help is in the name of the Lord, the Maker of heaven and earth.

Ps. 124:2–8 NIV

Discussion Questions

1. Is it easy to make new friends when you are in a new school?

2. How did standing up to a bully help Pam make new friends?

3. Does it always work that way?

4. In the Bible, read Job 29:11–12. Why was Job upset? (See Chapters 1 and 2 to discover Job's predicament.) Did he have a valid reason to be?

5. Do members of a team usually become friends? Why or why not?

6. What is the difference between playing on a sports team and being a member of a class?

7. Have you ever felt angry because people misunderstood you? If so, how did you react?

8. Do you think it is healthy to express anger in ways that do not hurt others?

9. In the Bible, read Psalm 37:8. How does anger turn into evil actions?

10. Pam mentioned shooting spitballs in class. What kinds of things do you remember doing in class to act up?

11. What benefits are there from having a job with responsibilities?

12. What did Pam see as the benefits of cleaning the lunchroom?

13. Why was Ruth considered a good friend?

14. In the Bible, read Philippians 2:3–4. How well did Ruth follow these instructions?

15. If everyone followed these instructions, would that make our world a better place?

Let's Talk
about withdrawal

Withdrawal is described as that state where the individual does not interact with other people well or at all. It may be physical, by not wanting to be in the same room with others; or it may be mental, where although in close proximity with others, the victim does not interact unless coaxed into answering simple questions. The answers are often short and to the point, often no more than a yes or no.

The causes for withdrawal are many and vary from person to person, but the most common cause is a feeling of inferiority. The individual has convinced himself that he or she is not intelligent enough or skilled enough to participate in a conversation with others at their level of understanding. The inferiority complex is only aggravated by the harsh words others use to the victim or about him or her. Some react only mildly to the taunts and teasing. Others draw deeper into themselves, much like a turtle withdraws into its shell for protection.

Once a person has withdrawn into his or her shell, it feels more comfortable than exposing oneself to the hurtful feeling of rejection. That comfort, although a false feeling, becomes a safe haven for the victim, and so he uses it whenever he feels threatened by others, either verbally or physically.

Withdrawal itself is not necessarily bad. In fact, it is good for anyone to get away once in a while to be alone with his or her thoughts or to just unwind from a busy day. It's what happens while a person is alone that may develop into a bad situation. Isolation leads to sessions of self-inspection and evaluation. That, in turn, may lead to a situation where the person convinces herself that everyone else is right and she is of no value. This may lead to self-torment or self-destruction. It is not uncommon for people to turn to drugs and alcohol, self-mutilation, or eating disorders to deal with the pain of rejection they feel so deeply.

Bill did not seem to fit into the circle of classmates he thought would make him happy. The others would call him names and use his desire to please to their advantage. Some of them knew Bill had easy access to beer at home, so they would talk him into giving them some. They seldom invited him to parties, and even when they were together, he felt alone. At some point, Bill started drinking when he was alone and eventually became an alcoholic. He died a horrible death in a car accident.

Janie was withdrawn most of her high school years due to teasing about her looks, her clothes, and her family, all things she could do nothing about. One day after an especially agonizing episode of self-reflection, she went to the river and jumped off the bridge.

We say our words do not hurt, but we really do not know the extent of the pain we inflict with our words.

The Bible teaches us that we should befriend the friendless. That means the kid who can't play softball well should still be included. Which is more important— winning the game or saving a life? Which is better—pushing a student aside telling him he's not good enough or including him and thus helping to improve his social skills?

The fact is withdrawn people almost never come out of their shell on their own. They need someone to come alongside of them to offer them friendship, concern, and help.

Pam was fortunate because she had someone who introduced her to an awareness of God early in her life. It was the idea that God cared for her that kept her going and gave her a sense of worth and hope. Not everyone has that. Actually most people do not. So, without your help, they are faced with the same hopelessness as Bill and Janie. Life has no meaning and offers little in the way of hope, so why go on living?

If you already know about God's love and concern for you, share it with someone who needs the same hope you have. You could potentially save a life. Now, wouldn't that feel great?

Chapter Three

High School and Beyond

When they had rowed for three or three and a half miles,
they were terrified.

John 6:19

But now high school was looming. Would I do as well? Would I be rewarded for my accomplishments there like I was in junior high? Would I have some of the same opportunities to play sports and compete in track and field events? I was scared of what the new environment would mean to me, but I was confident that I would get through it somehow, someway.

In September 1973, I was introduced to high school life. As you know, high school is like no other phase in anyone's life. It is where you really begin to find out who you are as a person, what you can accomplish as a student, and what standing you have as an athlete. In high school, you are challenged to do things that you might never think of doing on your own. Here the teachers no longer feed you information and expect you to learn it. Instead you are asked to develop study habits that require you to think on your own and to research subjects and write papers.

For me, it was a little different because I was still kept apart from the main body of students due to my handicaps. I continued to meet in small classes with other special-needs students with teachers who were trained to work with us. The main thing that was different now was that we had a different teacher for each subject instead of one teacher all day.

Academically there was little change for me until about halfway through my junior year. At that time, it was decided that as many special-needs students as possible would be integrated into the "mainstream" classes. This meant I had to be with the general population and try to learn along with them. That was not easy. Mainstreaming was introduced gradually, which helped me a lot. As each class was transformed, I soon realized my strengths and weaknesses. I was good at math and did all right in some subjects, but had to really struggle with reading and history. My favorite class was phys ed. I loved the activity and the relief from thinking, reading, and the closeness of the classroom. Phys ed gave me an opportunity to be me without much pressure to perform or do well. We learned to play all kinds of sports, but were not expected to be outstanding players.

It was through sports that I began to shine. Having done so well at the eighth-grade field day, I was eager to see how well I would do here among older, stronger kids.

My field hockey high school career began in an unusual way. Tryouts had already been held and the roster set, but a friend of mine, who had witnessed my performance in junior high, asked the coach to give me a chance, so I was asked to come to the next practice to see what I could do. I was a little nervous. However, as soon as that ball came my way, I was on fire. I outplayed the one girl who everyone thought was the best. Impressed by my skills, the coach put me on the junior varsity team. Soon there was an opening on varsity, and I was moved up.

This was both good and bad. It was good for the team to have my skills added to the other good players'. It was bad in the sense that the old feelings of rejection came flooding back.

The school had issued a fixed number of playing jerseys, so either someone had to give up a jersey to me or I had to play out of uniform. Since no one wanted to step aside to allow me to be fully accepted on the team by giving me a jersey, I felt a little hurt. I felt those old feelings of being not welcome. But now I had a purpose. I was now fifteen years old and resolved to show the world I was worthy of being one of them. The fact that the one girl who was asked to give me a jersey refused to do so did not set me back. I went home and put together a jersey that was as similar to theirs as I could make it. It was apparent that it was different, but close enough to be accepted by the coach.

I played all four years of high school with that jersey. Although it made me stand out among the others, I accepted it for what it was. It was a symbol of bigotry and prejudice for some. It was a symbol of triumph for others. It took me a long time to be fully integrated into the team. I never made captain, but I did eventually gain the respect of the other players.

I loved to run. Outside of school, I would run. Whenever an opportunity came, I would run. So when the Special Olympics were presented to us and I was chosen to represent my school at the games in Michigan, guess which event I chose. I would run the one mile event and love it. I guess one of the reasons I loved to run long distances was because while I was running I could talk things over in my head. I could ask questions and try to come up with reasonable answers. I didn't always find the answers though. As many questions went unanswered as were answered. But still, I was able to be alone with my thoughts.

While in Michigan, I received a trophy for doing well in an event I had not planned to enter: softball throwing. That not only pleased me, but when I arrived home, they threw a party for me and cheered my success. Having the support and encouragement of my family and friends pleased me very much.

In my senior year, my life took another dramatic turn. My dad got real sick and couldn't work anymore. I had to find a way to bring an income into our family to help pay the bills as well as continue my education. Fortunately, there were people willing to step in and help with that. One of my teachers arranged for me to work at the school three hours a day after classes as a custodian. This brought me pay through an agency of the state of Maine. It was not great pay, but it helped. When summer came, the hours increased, as did the size of my paycheck.

It was also in my senior year that I had my first date. A boy that I had had my eye on asked me to go to the prom with him, and I accepted. To be asked to the biggest dance of the year was special to me. I looked forward to it with great anticipation. But whoever started the rumor that it was the best thing going was wrong. When I got there, I found that it was really no different here than anywhere else. All the students grouped themselves as they normally did in the hallways at school. Certain ones hung out with other certain ones, without mixing to any extent. The tables were arranged to seat small groups, and if you didn't fit into a group, you'd better not try to sit at their table. The whole scene made me feel very self-conscious. To his credit, my date tried to make me feel comfortable while we were there.

Graduation was a different story. All throughout my school years, people teased me about not being able to get my diploma. My sister was one of the main ones in that effort. Every time she saw my report card, she would say demeaning things about my progress. But the closer graduation came, the more they understood that I was not going to quit. As it turned out, I was only the second person in my family to graduate from high school. Boy, was I proud that day. I was even more excited that my dad lived to see me graduate. With his struggle with emphysema, there were times when we didn't know how much longer he would last. To see him in the crowd was a real blessing to me.

I had a major decision to make shortly after the ceremony. Some of the students had planned a graduation party, to which many of us went. It was fun for a while, but soon the alcohol began to flow and drugs were introduced. It was their way of trying to keep the exhilaration of graduation alive for a few more hours. For me, it didn't work. I was disgusted with their behavior and wanted no part of it. I called my dad, who came to get me out of there. I convinced myself that if I had struggled so long and hard to make something of my life, I would not lower myself, not even for one night, to such a level just to fit in with others. I would be a loner for life before I would do that.

While all these things were going on, I had drifted away from the Lord. I rarely went to church and certainly did not pray very often. I still spent time with my grandmother Houghton. I would go to her house occasionally to help with chores or other things that needed to be done, and she continued to share Bible verses with me and let me know she was praying for me. Spiritually I was almost in the same situation as I was socially. Not many people cared about me, and I didn't care much to be with them. I was alone to try to find my way.

By the way, don't do what I did. If you have godly parents or grandparents, listen to them. Make their faith your faith. It will serve you well. See 2 Timothy 1:5–7. That's one of the first lessons any person who comes from a Christian home needs to learn. You cannot get to heaven on your parent's or grandparent's faith according to Ezekiel 18:20.

After graduation, I was in the same position as most recent graduates. I had to either find a job or go to college to earn a degree. Since I had struggled all through school up to this point, I was not what you might call "college material." So I found a few odd jobs to do that first summer, moving from one job to another for a while and finally getting regular work at Bass Shoe.

Even though I had decided not to accept the lifestyle of alcohol and drugs at graduation time, I slowly began to include drinking and smoking in my daily habits. In spite of my earlier feelings that they did not really help a person find real friends, I was doing the very thing I said I would not do. My conscience said one thing; my mind said another. I chose to follow the faulty reasoning in my mind.

Things went on this way for a while until one day some of my "friends" thought it would be fun to take sexual advantage of me. This left me feeling dirty, ashamed, and weak. I went to my brother's house, took a shower, and again told myself that this was not the direction I wanted my life to go in. But where could I turn? Who could help?

The Lord is so extremely patient with us, isn't he? There was a lady who worked with me at my job who often spoke to me about the Lord and urged me to go to church. She even offered to help me with my reading and comprehension skills. Up until now, I had kindly refused. I didn't think it would really make much difference.

About ten years after high school, after wasting my life with tobacco and alcohol and after having been sexually molested, I finally came to the conclusion that I was an alcoholic and needed to change. I could see that if I continued on this path, I would end up just like everyone had said I would—a loser.

Shortly after coming to that conclusion, I started meeting with my friend from work, who had volunteered to help me with my reading skills and personally teach me about Christianity. We sometimes met in her home reading from the Bible and discussing what the verses that we read meant. Other times we would meet at my parent's home where I still maintained a room. That summer I began attending the church where she worshipped and her father was the pastor. My life, for the first time, was beginning to show positive changes. It was while I was attending her church that I took the step to be baptized. Like so many others, I thought baptism would change me and make me a better person. This feeling continued until my friend chose to go off to college in the fall. Even though she looked me up every time she came home to visit, I began to go back to my old ways of living. This went on for the four years she was away. After graduation, she moved away and I lost touch with her. Would I ever find the solid rock I need for an anchor in my life?

Someone who did have a solid anchor, however, was my dad. About the time I graduated from high school, he became a Christian. One of his prayers, after knowing how wonderful it is, was that all of his family, including his children and grandchildren, would also come to be saved through Jesus. He shared this desire with his pastor just before he died in 1981.

The Lord is a refuge for the oppressed, a stronghold in times of trouble. Those who know your name will trust in you, for you, Lord, have never forsaken those who seek you.

Ps. 9:9–10 NIV

Discussion Questions

1. If you are already in high school (or beyond), what was the biggest difference for you from what you experienced before?

2. If you are not yet in high school, what do you anticipate as a major change for you?

3. Were there or are there any special-needs students in any of your classes?

4. How well did they participate in class discussions or activities? How did that make you feel?

5. In your opinion, do special-needs students make good athletes? Why or why not?

6. Pam talked about not being given an official jersey to play field hockey. Could that happen at your school? Why or why not?

7. One girl was asked to give a jersey to Pam and she refused. Would that be tolerated in your school?

8. What was wrong with her attitude?

9. Have you ever asked yourself questions about life and not found the answers?

10. Where do you believe someone should go to find answers? Are there some questions that have no answers?

11. Dating can be awkward for anyone. How is it more so for people with disabilities?

12. In your opinion, is the school prom a good choice for a first date? Why or why not?

13. What made the graduation party disgusting for Pam?

14. How much are you aware of drugs and alcohol among your classmates?

15. Pam says she rejected these things at first, but later found herself drinking and smoking. How do you suppose this happened?

16. Is what happened to Pam unusual? Has it happened to you?

17. In the Bible, read Proverbs 20:1 and 23:29–35. What does it say about drinking

alcohol? The same thing applies to drugs, doesn't it?

18. How can going to church with your family help you deal with bad habits?

19. Is there someone in your life who has offered to read the Bible with you or help you understand God? If yes, call them and say you want to learn more. If not, call a local church and ask to speak to the pastor.

20. Pam experienced the value of having a friend read, pray, and study with her. Why is this important?

21. Do you find it easier to study with someone else?

22. What can we do if our study mate moves away?

23. In the Bible, read Proverbs 18:24. Who is the author talking about?

24. Do you have Him as your friend?

Let's Talk
about fear

Fear has many sources. Some are valid; some are not. To be afraid of falling from a platform many feet above the ground is a valid fear. Fearing injury if you play tag is not so valid. Whatever the source and however valid the fear may be, every person's fear is real. Real fear triggers real reactions that are usually not good for the psychological welfare of the individual.

In the case of someone who has been taunted regularly for years, the fear of rejection is rehearsed over and over again. The result is either a hardening to the harsh words or a mental torment that leads to further deterioration of the victim's self-image. The perpetrator may not realize that the words said to the victim are so demeaning. But for the receiver, they are like a knife penetrating to the very heart and soul of his being.

It is one thing to try to scare a girl with a snake or frog waved in her face. It is truly another thing to scare that same girl by telling her she is of no value or incapable of doing the same things you do. For her, the rejection is much more damaging than the temporary presence of a reptile. The reptile will soon be gone and the incident over. The slurs will remain in her memory for a long time, perhaps even for life.

Fear of rejection is what has caused many students to fail to volunteer in class for projects or to participate in sports. Many capable individuals have been prevented from contributing to the welfare of the school and community because they are held back by a fear of rejection, a fear that is rooted in the way they are perceived and treated by their peers.

Mistreatment also triggers fear of physical harm. Anyone who is honest with herself will tell you that she has witnessed physical harm that came to someone as a result of mistreatment due to handicap, race, gender, or some other criteria. The harm varies from the not-so-gentle shove in the cafeteria line to actual beating up of the victim. There have actually been cases where murder has occurred. So those who are victims of slurs, remarks of hatred, degrading comments, or similar remarks have a justifiable reason to fear their tormentors. When they experience shoving, tripping, or grabbing of their books in the hallway, they fear that the next time it might be something worse. They are afraid that if the bully should happen to meet them off school grounds with no adults present, the level of violence might escalate.

Fears are very difficult, if not impossible, to overcome. Some fears are actually healthy. The fear of the high platform, for example, keeps you from going too close to the edge and endangering yourself. Unhealthy fears, however, may plague us our entire lives, and in far too many cases they cripple the victim to the point of incapacity. Fear of rejection and fear of physical abuse from peers are unhealthy fears. But because they are so ingrained in a person's life and environment, they cannot be erased. They can only be controlled.

How can the victim of such fears gain control of the fear and use that control to make life better for himself and others around him?

First, the victim must recognize the fear for what it is. It is a reaction to what others are saying or doing to us. To gain control over this kind of fear, we must remember that every person is created by God as special and unique. Once we accept that as fact, we can also accept the fact that we are valuable as we are. Our value as a person does not depend on what others say or think about us. Our value does not depend on how much we can contribute to society. Our value does not hinge on our grade point average or class standing. The value of an individual is determined solely by his existence. Anyone and everyone who is alive has value and is worthy of respect and equal treatment.

There is no race that is superior to another. There is no inequality between the genders. There is no cause for mistreatment due to handicaps or mental illnesses. Age should not be an excuse for discrimination. If we all believed the truth that we are created equal in the sight of our Creator, then we would learn to treat one another with more tolerance, more dignity, and more acceptance in spite of our differences.

Now, once a person has a solid grip on the fact that we are all valuable, then the next step is to try to make life better for someone else. As a victim, a person can truly understand what another victim is going through. Because of that, someone who understands that she has worth can go to another victim and show compassion, comradeship, and encouragement. Because someone is or has been the victim of bullying, taunting, and teasing, who better to stand with another victim and thus increase his own self-worth? God sees us as valuable in our own right, but He also sees a tremendous value in helping someone else in his or her time of trouble. In fact, if you may recall, the very reason that Eve was made was to "be a helpmate for him." One of the very purposes for our existence as individuals is to be a help to anyone we can with the ability and resources we have available to us. That is where a major part of our value as a human lies.

Have you mistreated others in the past? Stop and consider that they are just as valuable as you. Try instead to treat them with equality, dignity, and value.

Have you been the victim? Use your experience as a tool to reach out to others to help them overcome the very real fears they have as a result of their situations. You can do it. Who knows, maybe God brought you to this place for this very reason: to help others the way you would have wanted someone to help you.

Chapter Four

Continuing the Struggle

He saw the disciples straining at the oars, because the wind was against them.

Mark 6:48 NIV

My employment at the shoe factory lasted for fourteen years. I had settled into a routine that was not much different from that of any factory worker. You get up, go to work, go home, relax a few hours, and then go to bed. Each day was a repeat of the one before it. No wonder most people in that situation begin, at some point, to live for the weekend. It was only then that you felt you had any control over your life.

When the shoe factory closed, I found work at Highland Lumber, driving a forklift. It was a much better job than being inside the factory for eight hours a day. This, however, required me to take a driver-safety course. *Here I am again,* I thought. Even though the other crew members did not know the severity of my handicap and the difficulty I had with reading comprehension, my boss did. She took great care to see that I understood the requirements of the job and was concerned when I did not make it known to my tester that I had a hard time with the written portion. Later, during a required hearing test, I gave a wrong answer and it was apparent to everybody. When a coworker heard about it he taunted me mercilessly. That made me mad at myself, at my inability, at the unfairness of it all. That old fear of failure reared its ugly head again. But knowing I could drive that forklift as well as anybody else helped put those feelings behind me once again. I worked in that lumberyard for four years and drove the lift with the best of them.

The worst part of driving a forklift in a lumberyard is the weather. Sunshine, rain, snow, high heat, freezing cold, or any combination thereof did not matter. The work had to be done. So I did it. But there comes a point when a person says enough is enough.

I took my third job at a local convenience store and gas station. Here I did pretty much what you would expect to be done in such a place. I stocked shelves, ran the register, pumped gas, and did whatever else needed to be done. It was while I was working there that I had opportunities to advance in my career. I moved up to floor person and later to assistant manager. As you can imagine, each new step upward came with its own challenges for me. I could operate the cash register easily enough. I could do the manual labor requirements without trouble; but when reading instructions was necessary, I usually failed to understand them. The tech support team at the home office used to get very upset with me because I would call them for help with matters that most other people could do easily. Once again, help was provided for me to assist me with my reading skills. This time I was responsible for paying toward the tutoring. My initial test to begin this new round of tutoring revealed that, even after all these years, I was reading at the third-grade level. So, even though it was not required for the job I had I felt it was necessary for me to continue receiving help.

I had a wonderful tutor who read with me and helped me read by breaking words into syllables. This was the one most helpful thing for me. I was soon reading whole books with her and at home on my own. But alas, it didn't last. After five years on the job, it was decided to close the store, and since I could not afford to continue it also meant the end of my tutoring.

With no job prospects lined up, I just drifted for a few months, living off my severance pay. I didn't know where I would go or what would happen to me. Thoughts of my old friend from the shoe shop crept back into my mind. With memories of her in my head, I would often think of how good it was when I was close to the Lord. But, unfortunately, they were fleeting thoughts and bore no fruit. After six months, I began working at Ellis' Market pumping gas.

This new part-time work was not really what I wanted to do with my life, and it required a lot of walking back and forth from the pump to the store and from the store to the pump. Back and forth, all day long. It was not long before I started having pains in my legs. I had them checked out by my doctor. After running several tests, it was discovered that my right hip was deteriorating even at my (relatively) young age. It was not thought severe enough to require hip replacement, so I was put on a regimen of pills to control the pain. After another six months I realized that the pain was just too much and my employment came to an end.

Thankfully, a custodial position opened up at the very grammar school I had attended earlier. This was also part-time but the stress on my hips would not be as great, plus the pay was higher than at the store, so my income increased. Not long after beginning this new venture, I found out that the custodial position could be combined with bus driving responsibilities.

To do both would make it a full-time job. I also discovered that my former tutor from many years earlier was still working at the school; still volunteering to help students part-time. We reconnected and she helped me a great deal to pass the necessary tests to become a bus driver. I could have chosen not to take the tests, but they were necessary to go full-time.

Fear and anxiety set in, as they had so many times before, but with her coaching me, I did well enough. I remember distinctly the review cards she made, the careful detail to reading skills, and the confidence boosters she gave me often. When it came time for the actual test, she was allowed to read it to me, which helped a lot as well.

My boss understood my situation because he was an old classmate of mine, familiar with my history. He took it upon himself to find other drivers who were willing to teach me the proper operation a school bus. But before any of them could do much, he changed his mind. Instead, he sent me to a vocational rehabilitation agency in Rumford that tested people to determine if they were qualified to receive funding to pay for the bus driving course. I qualified and was soon mired in the process which was actually good for me. Now I found myself in a time-crunch situation. I would go to work and meet my responsibilities, attend bus driver training classes, connect with my tutor to try to improve my reading and comprehension skills, and then go home and study for the exam. This didn't leave me much time to think about my life. Because of the heavy work load I didn't have much time to dwell on my shortcomings.

The feelings of inferiority never go away—not because a person chooses to dwell on them, but mostly because other people keep reminding you of your handicap. I had proven to my family and friends that I could graduate from high school. I had shown my coach and other athletes that I could play with the best. I had done well at all my previous jobs. Yet the stigma of not being average or above kept getting thrown in my face. I was regularly teased, and people still tried to tell me I couldn't succeed. One of my uncles was among the few who believed in me. Once again, I had to prove myself to them. Once again, I had to work harder and do better than anyone else to be accepted.

I distinctly remember an incident during this time that really made me upset. At work one day, my shoelace had come untied, as happens to everyone now and then. A fellow worker pointed it out to me with very sarcastic remarks. "Are you from Carthage? Are you so stupid you can't tie your shoe?" This really offended me, but I kept my thoughts to myself and suppressed my anger. Later, I considered the unfairness of it and reported the incident to the personnel office. I made it clear that I felt I worked almost twice as hard as anyone else and deserved some respect for my skills.

As a result of this incident and others like it, I was diagnosed with anxiety. I would have spells where my heart would begin racing, I would break out in a sweat and feel lightheaded, and I would try to find a place of solitude. I didn't want to be around anyone else at that time. I was prescribed some medication, which helped a lot. It got so bad at times that I would have to give myself pep talks just before going to work. I would sit in my car in the parking lot and tell myself, "You can do this. You will get through the day. Whatever they say, you are better than that," and other similar statements. Memories of old school days would come flooding back. Looking at the building and thinking of all the struggles I faced back then, I realized that it hadn't gotten much easier at all after so many years. Had I known how to pray, I certainly would have, but that habit was gone a long time before.

My persistence and hard work finally paid off. During the course work in preparation for driving a school bus, I earned several awards that showed me that it was worth it. I was named "Best

Student" and "Most Improved Student," and I was awarded a certificate for perfect attendance. But the best award was the certificate of completion I was given at the end of the course. I had passed! As soon as I received that paper, I called my uncle. He was so proud of me.

So I began my career as a custodian/ bus driver. My driving opportunities were few at first. Being new to the staff, I was assigned substitution status, which meant I would only drive when another driver couldn't for some reason. That was okay since I needed time to develop my bus-driving skills anyway. Later, when a full-time bus route opened up, I took it. Wouldn't you know? My first route took me to the homes of my neighbors and former schoolmates in my hometown.

I hit it off with the kids right away. I learned to tell when one of my regulars was having a hard day or was struggling with being accepted. Believe me, it shows on a child's face and in the way she carries herself. Knowing what it is like firsthand, I could identify easily.

There were many opportunities to speak to my young bus riders about being respectful, considerate, and understanding. Whenever I heard unkind words, I would make it a point to talk about how that makes a person feel when he or she is the victim. I felt that my life experiences were being used in a positive way and that it was not all in vain.

The kids on my bus soon learned that I truly loved them and would stand up for them when they had needs or were being treated unfairly. By the end of that first school year, they had begun to love me as well. I knew how to relate to these kids because I knew what I had needed in such situations when I was their age. Was God using me even then? I don't know. Perhaps.

All this time, my bone degeneration continued. I was in pain a lot. At one point, my right knee required restorative surgery. I had trouble walking and doing my job at the school and driving the bus. Finally, after two years, I had to give it up. I could no longer be on my feet for very long at a time, and driving became a very painful experience. The first thoughts that came to me after making that decision were thoughts of discouragement. *Am I getting knocked down again? Why is my life such a challenge when I see so many others seemingly having an easy time? Where is God in all of this?*

I am in pain and distress; may your salvation, O God, protect me . . . . I pray to you, O Lord, in the time of your favor; in your great love, O God, answer me with your sure salvation. Rescue me from the mire, do not let me sink; deliver me from those who hate me, from the deep waters.

Ps. 69: 29, 13 - 14

Discussion Questions

1. Does it surprise you that Pam, as an adult with a reading and writing handicap, worked in the kinds of jobs she did?

2. Along the way, Pam received help from other caring adults. Why was this important to her?

3. In what other ways can caring adults help people with handicaps?

4. At what age should people begin to receive help in job training?

5. When Pam got upset over the shoelace incident, was she right to report it to the authorities?

6. Was there another, better way to deal with the one who offended her?

7. In the Bible, read Matthew 18:15–16. How does Jesus say we should handle such a situation?

8. What made Pam's bus-driving position special for her?

9. Pam says she felt her life experiences helped her identify well with the kids on her bus. Is there any life experience you have had that may help you understand someone else's situation?

10. In the Bible, read 2 Corinthians 1:1–7. For what reason did Paul say some people suffer hardships?

11. Could this include handicaps?

12. At the end of this chapter, Pam is feeling discouraged because of all her pain in addition to her handicap. Do you sometimes feel discouraged? If so, why?

13. In the Bible, read Psalm 20. To whom did the writer go for comfort and courage?

14. How do the verses from another psalm quoted at the end of the chapter fit your situation?

15. If you have not talked to God about your problems, why not start now?

Let's Talk

about discouragement

By the time a handicapped person has reached adulthood, he has been the victim of slurs, bad jokes, and intentionally disparaging remarks for far too long. In some cases, the negative attitude began almost as soon as they were born. A lifetime of hearing these things can really become infectious in a person's brain.

In every one of us, there is a breaking point at which we give up. We no longer try to stand up against the forces of evil. We do not resist the negative thoughts and remarks; and often victims begin to embrace them, believe them, and accept as truth the lies they have been hearing for so long.

When this happens, it is the direct result of discouragement. Discouragement sets in when there seems to be no way out, no source of help or hope, no becoming the kind of person others will accept as their equal.

Discouragement, if not remedied, leads to disaster. The remedy for discouragement is for a human being with a caring heart to come alongside of the victim to encourage him, pray with him, and get him to see his personal value and worth to others in his home, school, church, or community. A good friend is a valuable asset to anyone, but more so to those who need an extra measure of hope.

Left unchecked, discouragement leads to a worsening of the victim's condition and possibly death. Withdrawal symptoms intensify, unwillingness to participate grows stronger, resistance to group activities increases, and the concept of personal self-worth goes through the floor. Many victims of discouragement have isolated themselves to the point where it takes professional help to draw them out again.

Discouragement can also lead to declining school grades. Students who are already struggling to achieve may be convinced there is no need to try or to even complete assignments since they will not be accepted as equal to those of other classmates anyway. When a student gives up, that should be a red flag to teachers and parents. It is a clear sign that something other than a bad day is happening. Parents, teachers, and other caring adults should then step in and work with the victim to bring her back to her normal place of participation and involvement.

A more serious result of discouragement is suicide. It is not at all unusual for individuals who have suffered at the hands of inconsiderate, racist, or prejudiced people for many years to end the suffering through death.

Susan was such a victim. From as early as she could remember, people had always called her names, teased her about the way she looked, bullied her at school, and mistreated her at work. It got so bad she often refused to go to work, knowing it would be torturous to spend the day with fellow workers who picked on her constantly. One day when she was feeling particularly down, she walked out of the house to be alone. They found her body a few hours later in the woods hanging from a tree. It was the only way she knew to end the fear, anxiety, and shame that others had placed on her.

The answer to discouragement is encouragement. As we have shown already, the way to counter discouragement is for a caring individual to come to the aid of the victim. That means all of us need to develop a more caring attitude toward others in general and to the handicapped in particular. It also means we need to be acutely aware of our own words and actions so that they do not contribute to the negative treatment of such people. The Bible teaches that we should always be looking at others with a positive attitude and be ready to praise them, lift them up, and say kind things about them, rather than the opposite. (See Philippians 4:8 and Romans 15:1–2.)

Everyone has experienced discouragement at one point or another.

We all know what it is like to feel like we did not or cannot succeed in reaching a goal. Since we know this from a temporary basis, we must consider how much more deep the feeling is when it is a long-term reality. A temporary discouragement may be overcome by another chance, additional teaching or practice, getting help from some outside source, or whatever it takes. A seemingly permanent feeling of despair will take much more to conquer. It will require you and me to change the way we view and treat others on a daily basis. If we, together, can adopt the biblical approach of looking for the positive side of people, those individuals we come in contact with will be lifted in their spirit, encouraged in their heart, and able to see the future in a whole new and brighter way. Who knows? Perhaps you will even save a life.

Chapter Five

Life Goes On

Then he climbed into the boat with them,
and the wind died down.

Mark 6:51 NIV

Where is God? That thought just wouldn't go out of my head. Why have all these difficulties happened in my life? Why me? Why do others have it so easy and I struggle for everything I have accomplished?

As a part of my postsurgical therapy, I would go for walks a lot. It was on these walks that I did a lot of thinking. It was an opportunity to be alone with my thoughts, and like it or not, for God to speak to me. I would pour out my complaints and share my broken heart, thinking that somehow He might hear me and respond. God is always ready to listen to us when we call out to Him. I just didn't realize how much he cared for me at that moment. Psalm 147:3–5 says: "He heals the brokenhearted and binds up their wounds. Great is our Lord and mighty in power; his understanding has no limit."

One time while walking, talking, and thinking about my life, it seemed that God spoke to me—perhaps not out loud, but to my heart and mind. I felt like he was telling me, "Don't be ashamed of anything that has happened to you or the struggles you have faced. I made you the way you are. The most important thing in life is Me and your relationship to Me. Get that straight, and other things will fall into line."

Shortly after that, my sister Mary talked to me a little bit about the Lord and expressed a desire to start a home Bible study. I only knew one person who might do it. My niece's husband was preparing for the ministry. Unfortunately, circumstances prevented him from taking on the responsibility. Our other sister, Brenda, suggested her pastor, who had become the leader of a Pentecostal church. As it turned out, her pastor was another old classmate from way back. At the studies, he helped me feel accepted and comfortable as we read and discussed various Scripture passages.

All the attendees were members of my family. That, too, felt good. Looking around the room, I felt like God was finally blessing my whole family, not just me. We studied with the Pentecostal pastor for almost a year. My relationship with the Lord was cemented and grew greatly during that time. At the end of the study, we were all baptized, I for the second time. This was a moment of true surrender to the Lord. I now understood more clearly what He did for me and what it means to submit to Him as Lord.

I believe that this was the hand of God again. There always seemed to be someone available to meet my current need exactly when I needed it. God's timing is never wrong. He knew that now I was ready to give my life over to Him. "Repent, then, and turn to God, so that your sins may be wiped out, that times of refreshing may come from the Lord, and that he may send the Christ, who has been appointed for you—even Jesus" (Acts 3:19–20).

There was one problem, however. I still smoked—a lot. I was up to a two-pack-a-day habit. How was I going to live for God and feed this craving for cigarettes?

Sometime during the course of the yearlong Bible study, I started attending the Pentecostal church. At one of their special services, I felt the Lord tell me to place my cigarettes on the altar in sacrifice to Him. I resisted for a short while, but knew that if I didn't, I was being disobedient to Him. So I made my way to the front and laid my pack on that altar, rejoicing that God had set me free! I have never smoked since. When Christ sets us free, we are free forever!

I soon learned that the Christian life is not without its own challenges. There are issues that even devout followers of God disagree on and that sometimes cause rifts and hard feelings. One such challenge came a little while after I had given up my smoking habit. There was a special speaker who was supposedly holding healing services at our church. During one of the sessions, he declared that I had been healed of my pain and suffering. Immediately after the service was over, my pastor took me into his office and counseled me that it might not be so. Who was right? Did God heal through this man or not? Why couldn't they agree on something so important?

I was also very uncomfortable with the concept of speaking in tongues. I hadn't learned a lot about it yet, but I knew that it just didn't feel right. I took it upon myself to do a Bible search on the subject and concluded that the instruction was clear that if it were to be practiced in public, there should be a translator present. It seemed to me they were abusing the practice to make the service more emotional.

There were other issues, mostly personal, with that church, so after a few months, I withdrew and started attending the church just down the road from my house. I soon discovered that controversy and disagreements are a way of life. That congregation was dealing with internal issues as well. Personally, I was faced with another challenge to be accepted. These people grew up with me. They knew my past. They knew what I had faced. Unfortunately, some of them were not willing to accept me for who I am today. That's okay. I know where I stand with God, and I know God isn't finished with me yet.

Here I am at more than fifty years old and loving my Lord more each day. The storms of life may have knocked me down many times, but God had a plan and a purpose for my life (Jer. 29:11). Just like the disciples in the boat on the Sea of Galilee, I have been in danger of sinking many times. But, praise God, Jesus was there to calm the storm. He stilled the waters and brought me safe to harbor. God was always there, whether or not I knew it or admitted it. He was working on me all that time to prepare me for what lies ahead. I don't know what the future holds for me, but I do know this: no matter what happens, Jesus and I will always be together from now on.

I want to leave you with this thought: God loves everyone as individuals, even though each one is different. He made you special, and He has a plan for you. Don't ignore Him when he calls you or wants to help you. He only has good things in mind for you and your future.

Sometimes you don't feel very special. You say something stupid in class. You look in the mirror and see a giant zit on the end of your nose. You? Special? You bet! You're a human being totally special to God (Gen. 1:27). You are a human being made in the image and likeness of God. Oh, you'll get zits and maybe you'll say a stupid thing or two, but don't let things like that rob you of feeling special, because you are!

Listen to God, not other people. Follow Him. He will lead you right and in the end will accept you into glory. Amen.

For you created my inmost being; you knit me together in my mother's womb. I praise you because I am fearfully and wonderfully made; your works are wonderful, I know that full well. My frame was not hidden from you when I was made in the secret place. When I was woven together in the depths of the earth, your eyes saw my unformed body. All the days ordained for me were written in your book before one of them came to be.

Ps. 139:13–16a

Discussion Questions

1. Do you go for walks or spend time alone? If so, what kinds of thoughts come to you?

2. In your opinion, why did thoughts of God come to Pam on her walks?

3. Does a handicapped person have anything to be ashamed of? If so, what?

4. How can being involved in a discussion group or Bible study group help someone who has been badly treated?

5. Why was Pam concerned about her smoking habit?

6. What was the cure for her? Will that work for everyone?

7. Pam found her self-worth through meeting Jesus and letting him take control of her life. Have you?

Let's Talk

about how much God loves you

"God loves the people of the world so much that he sacrificed his only Son for you" (John 3:16).

You need to believe this as a fact.

Here's how you can have a real joy and purpose in life:

Admit that you are not perfect and have done bad things in your life (sins). (See Romans 3:23.)

Believe that Jesus can forgive you and set you free from guilt and punishment for those sins. (See John 3:18.)

Confess your sinfulness and helplessness to God, asking for His help. (See Romans 10:9–10.)

Determine to live in obedience to God and the principles He has written in the Bible from now on. (See Ephesians 2:10.)

Some Final Thoughts

Special education is not performed the same way today as it was when I was in school. Most students are integrated into the mainstream as much as possible. This has been a positive thing for the most part, because students are taught early to be accepting toward others with handicaps, whether physical or mental.

It is very important that people of all ages learn to be more accepting. No one asks for a handicap. Since they cannot help the condition they are in, we must learn to accept them for who they are. God did not make a mistake when He gave them the handicap they have. Since we are all creations of God, we must learn to accept one another as equally important in the sight of God.

From the other side of the coin, we must also be ready and willing to forgive those people who hurt us along the way. Many of them do not realize the truth of being equal with God. Many of them have prejudices and biases that affect their thinking. Without the Lord in their lives, they cannot understand what it means to truly forgive or be forgiven. Knowing these facts, anyone feeling bullied, harassed, picked on, or discriminated against should be extra careful to offer forgiveness.

On speaking in tongues: What I said earlier is in no way a slander on my brothers and sisters who are comfortable with this practice. I believe they are truly born again; we just have a different understanding of the purpose and use of tongues. If anyone is offended by my remarks, I sincerely apologize.

Pam Turner

Comments:

"Pam could have let the waves swamp her, but she has persevered with Jesus by her side."

Clemma Nichols

Church worker

Rumford First Baptist Church

"This delightful book teaches us the importance of and how to be nice to each other by being kind, gentle and filled with God's love."

Rev. Doug Forbes

Associate pastor

Central Congregational Church

Consultant, Gospel Light Publications